WITH THE WORD

A BIBLE STUDY AND DEVOTIONAL GUIDE
FOR GROUPS OR INDIVIDUALS

Faith & Life Resources

Harrisonburg, VA
Waterloo, ON

With the Word: Matthew
Copyright © 2012 by Faith & Life Resources, Harrisonburg, Virginia 22802
 Released simultaneously in Canada by Faith & Life Resources,
 Waterloo, Ontario N2L 6H7. All rights reserved.
International Standard Book Number: 978-0-8361-9639-9
Printed in United States of America
Edited by Eleanor Snyder, cover and interior design by Merrill R. Miller

Sessions from *Adult Bible Study Teacher* and *Adult Bible Study Student*, along with *Rejoice!* daily devotions were all used in the writing of *With the Word: Matthew*. *Believer's Church Bible Commentary: Matthew*, by Richard B. Gardner (Scottdale, Pa: Mennonite Publishing House, 1991) was consulted for some of the sessions.

All rights reserved. This publication may not be reproduced, stored in a retrieval system, or transmitted in whole or in part, in any form, by any means, electronic, mechanical, photocopying, recording or otherwise without prior permission of the copyright owners.

Scripture quotation taken from the Holy Bible, *New Revised Standard Version Bible*, copyright ©1989, Division of Christian Education of the National Council of the Churches of Christ in the United States of America. Used by permission. All rights reserved.

To order or request information, please call 1-800-245-7894 in the U.S. or 1-800-631-6535 in Canada. Or visit www.faithandliferesources.org.

16 15 14 13 12   10 9 8 7 6 5 4 3 2 1

Table of contents

INTRODUCTION
5

SESSION FORMAT
7

1. DARING OBEDIENCE (MATTHEW 1:18-25)
8

2. PROVOCATIVE PREACHER (MATTHEW 3:1-12)
14

3. DECLARING IDENTITY (MATTHEW 3:13-17)
20

4. FINDING TRUE HAPPINESS (MATTHEW 5:1-12)
26

5. SALT, LIGHT, ACTION! (MATTHEW 5:13-20)
32

6. REDEFINING THE RULES (MATTHEW 5:21-48)
38

7. PRACTICING PIETY AND TRUST (MATTHEW 6:1-15; 25-34)
44

8. MEETING HUMAN NEEDS (MATTHEW 2 5:31-46)
50

Introduction

* *

Welcome to With the Word! This exciting new series from Faith & Life Resources invites you to draw closer to God by spending time with the Word through Bible study and daily devotions.

Studying Matthew

In Matthew, there are three worlds to explore. And for each of these worlds, there are certain questions to raise or procedures to follow to discover what is going on.

The *world* of Matthew is, first of all, *the world we find within the story Matthew tells*. Like contemporary books, dramas, and filmscripts, the First Gospel plunges us into a miniature universe of speech and action. Certain characters play prominent roles in this literary world, characters such as Jesus, the disciples, Jewish leaders, and the crowds. Together with other characters, these persons take part in a developing plot, a plot marked by a growing conflict that eventually leads to Jesus' death.

The second *world* of Matthew is *the historical setting in which this Gospel was composed*. The story Matthew tells is not simply a piece of art for art's sake, but a text with vital connections to the real-life story of Christian groups in the first century. To begin with, the sources on which Matthew draws to construct his story came *from* the developing church. In a similar manner, Matthew writes *for* a community in time and space, readers shaped by a particular cultural heritage and facing critical issues in their social and religious context.

A still broader *world* which the First Gospel inhabits is *the story of the people of God from the days of Abraham and Sarah right down to our own time*. Although Matthew wrote to Christians in a particular time and place, his text is part of an ongoing conversation between God and the faith community. Earlier moments in this dialogue helped to shape Matthew's own script, and Matthew's script has played a key role in the conversation ever since.

> —from Richard B. Gardner, *Matthew*, Believers Church Bible Commentary (Scottdale, Pa.: Herald Press, 1991), 19-20. Used by permission.

Session format

In this volume on *Matthew*, you will find eight sessions for either group or individual use. The easy-to-use format starts with an in-depth Bible study and ends with seven short devotionals designed to be read in the days after the session. Here's a guide to each session:

- **Opening:** The opening of the Bible study portion calls you into the session through a summary of the text and a few questions for reflection. Before you begin each session, take time to read the text reflectively.
- **For the leader:** These are ideas for how to use the material in a group setting. If using the material individually, omit this section.
- **Understanding God's Word:** This section makes connections between the session's text and today's world.
- **Connecting with God's Word:** This is the heart of the guide; it's the in-depth Bible study that calls you to examine specific parts of the session's text. The writer gives background for a few verses of text, then outlines a series of questions for personal reflection or discussion. These questions always invite you to make connections between the biblical text and your own life.
- **Closing:** The Bible study portion of the session then closes with a brief time of worship and wrapping up.
- **Devotionals:** Immediately after the sessions you will find seven short devotionals on the session's text. Each devotional starts with a Scripture verse, includes a meditation, and ends with a prayer. Use these seven inspiring devotionals in the days after the session as way to keep the text in your heart and mind.

Spend time *With the Word* today!

Daring obedience

MATTHEW 1:18-25

Opening

Think of a time when you made a difficult decision. What were some positive and negative outcomes of your decision? Do you have regrets about your decision?

In Matthew 1 we learn that Joseph is not Jesus' biological father, but will raise him as his own. Joseph struggles to make the right decision in a difficult situation.

Understanding God's Word

Joseph is one of the New Testament's underappreciated heroes. He seems fated to take a back seat to the profound and poetic teenager he married. Nevertheless, there is much to admire about this careful, obedient, and dogged man. Caught up in events that are larger than history, troubled by dreams that order him to marry, to flee, to return and relocate, Joseph always rises in the morning with his face set toward obedience. In an unconventional act of daring obedience, he accepts God's call to play a supportive role in raising a child with a unique mission. Following the birth narratives, Joseph disappears from the Gospel's story.

For the leader

In keeping with the Matthew 1 text, invite people to tell something interesting about someone in their family lineage.

1. If this is the first gathering, talk about your expectations and hopes for the group.

2. Pray for openness to God's surprising and unpredictable movement in your life.

3. Have three readers (narrator, angel, prophet) read the text while others listen. Then invite each person to identify a key word or phrase that was meaningful. Do not discuss these words.

Connecting with God's Word

A righteous man (1:18-19)

This story begins with Joseph, a "righteous" man from Nazareth, facing an anguishing dilemma, which for him has no acceptable resolution. He is "pledged" to Mary, likely a teenage woman of the village. This betrothal is a formal agreement between the two families involved, the first stage of the marriage itself.

The marriage has been initiated, but Joseph and Mary have not yet consummated their relationship as husband and wife. In this time of high anticipation, Joseph discovers that Mary is pregnant. Joseph can only imagine the worst—Mary's unfaithfulness. Matthew tells his readers that Mary is pregnant "through the Holy Spirit." But all Joseph knows is that his wife is pregnant and he is not the father. Jewish law is clear about how to deal with such situations (Deuteronomy 22:23-27), and the legal outcomes are not kind.

There are no good answers in sight for Joseph. His "righteousness" obliges him to uphold the Jewish law. To be righteous means to be just, to do the right thing in a given situation. In this context it means that Joseph is not willing to subject Mary to public disgrace. He must treat everyone with compassion and respect, even one whom he suspects has betrayed him. There is only one option, as Joseph sees it—a quiet divorce. In reality, it would have been difficult for Joseph to do this. He and Mary lived in a small town where everyone knew everyone else's business. Perhaps this is why it took some time for Joseph to decide what to do.

Joseph's high standard of ethical conduct is grounded in the Hebrew Bible. It appears that he integrated what he learned, most probably, in the local synagogue. His behavior indicates that he has been schooled in the ethics of grace.

- Joseph struggles deeply with questions of morality, ethics, and personal identity. What struggles do we face in our world of complex and challenging realities?
- What are the habits of a "righteous" person living in our times?
- What would you include in a curriculum for teaching an "ethic of grace"?

Joseph's call (1:20-24)

Joseph changes his mind as a result of a dream. In ancient times, some people believed that God communicated through dreams. Joseph is told that he should not be afraid to take Mary to be his wife. Of what would he be afraid? Perhaps that she will be unfaithful to him in the future or that people would think that he was not as righteous as he appeared to be.

In formulaic language, Joseph is told about Mary's child and to name the child Jesus, which means, "he delivers (or saves)." The child will save people, not from Rome or outside enemies, but from their own sins, and from those things that prevent people from being fully what God intended them to be. Furthermore, this event represents a fulfillment of prophecy from the time of Isaiah, of the birth of a child who will be named Emmanuel. This symbolic name affirms the presence of God among God's people.

Joseph accepts the dream as God's word, marries Mary, and becomes a father to Jesus. He is not a major player in Matthew's Gospel but without him, the story of Jesus would be quite different. Joseph willingly plays a supporting role. The fine qualities that he displays make him an ideal dad for Jesus.

- Do you pay attention to your dreams? If so, how have dreams influenced your life?
- Identify individuals in your congregation who are fulfilling their calling to a supportive role. Are they being affirmed in meaningful ways?
- Sometimes it feels that our contributions are underappreciated or not recognized. How can we validate ourselves?

Daring Obedience (Matthew 1:24-25)

In this story, Joseph changes from a desperate man with an anguishing plan of action to an obedient man with a daring plan of action. What changes him? He hears the message of the angel, decides to trust God, and responds in obedience to God's call. It's a daring act to dream God's dreams and to awake into God's new reality. God's unconventional actions call for unconventional responses.

- How can we get ready for God's unpredictable and powerful actions in our world?
- What might God be calling you, your congregation or the wider church to dare to obey?

Closing

1. Joseph is a model for daring obedience. Share one insight you gained from this text that will help you live out your calling this week.

2. Give this sending blessing to each other: *Do not be afraid for God is among us. Dare to live boldly in God's new reality.*

Devotionals

Devotional 1

Her husband Joseph, being a righteous man and unwilling to expose her to public disgrace, planned to dismiss her quietly.
—Matthew 1:19

In *Mornings with Henri J. M. Nouwen*, Nouwen writes: "The blessed one always blesses. And people want to be blessed . . . No one is brought to life through curses, gossip, accusations or blaming . . . it calls forth only darkness, destruction and death. As 'the blessed ones' we can walk through the world and offer blessings."

Joseph's actions qualify him as a blessed one. In our age of scandalous talk shows and shocking news coverage, Joseph's behavior seems extraordinary. He believes God's angel who assures him that Mary's pregnancy is sacred, not scandalous, because she is carrying the very Son of God. He has the moral fiber and inner strength to take care of Mary in a dignified way no matter what the neighborhood thinks!

Do I have that same strength of character? How can I be one of the blessed ones today? *–Annie Lind*

Lord, you have blessed us with the gift of Jesus. May we bless those we meet today.

Devotional 2

Joseph, son of David, do not be afraid to take Mary as your wife, for the child conceived in her is from the Holy Spirit. —Matthew 1:20

I've always assumed this is a comforting dream for Joseph because it gave clear direction from God. The dream convinces Joseph that Mary has not been unfaithful. But what about everyone else in the village? Will they make fun of Joseph?

We may covet such clear direction, but we need to be prepared for what God might say. It may mean undertaking something that no one around us will understand. What if God asks you to quit your good job and go on a mission assignment? Or to act lovingly toward someone who has publicly humiliated you? Or to sell your house at a fraction of its cost to a refugee family?

God did a new thing in the lives of Joseph and Mary that changed the course of history. God specializes in setting directions, new directions. I wonder what we will be dreaming tonight. *–Carol Penner*

Giver of dreams, give us courage to follow the dreams you send.

Devotional 3

Joseph, son of David, do not be afraid to take Mary as your wife, for the child conceived in her is from the Holy Spirit. —Matthew 1:20

When Joseph learns of Mary's pregnancy, he is devastated and fearful. He does not know that God's Spirit has intervened in their lives for a special purpose. However, he may have been familiar with another conception story of divine intervention. At age 100, Abraham and 90-year-old Sarah learned from an angel that they would have a son.

God's intervention in Jesus' birth is even more amazing because Mary conceives without human involvement. This conception should not surprise us. In creation, the Spirit brought the material universe from nothing. God fashioned humans from the dust of the earth. Is it any more marvelous that God miraculously creates life in the womb of Mary, so it can be written, "The child within her has been conceived by the Holy Spirit"? –*Michael Dick*

God, we open ourselves to the miraculous power of your Spirit.

Devotional 4

Joseph, son of David, do not be afraid to take Mary as your wife, for the child conceived in her is from the Holy Spirit. —Matthew 1:20

In Jewish thought the Holy Spirit had a definite role: to bring God's truth to humankind and to serve as God's agent in renewing the soul. Matthew's account of the incarnation emphasizes that in Jesus the Spirit of God was operative in a powerful new way.

Jonah, a Chinese itinerant preacher, maintained an exhaustive schedule. He would carry 60 pounds of Bibles on his back as he cycled miles along bumpy roads to instruct house church leaders. On one visit he learned of a major dispute causing division in the congregation. He called the elders together. The atmosphere was tense as Jonah sat awhile in silence. Then, in tears, he cried, "Oh Lord, how we have dirtied your name."

Soon others began weeping. Conviction of sin, followed by repentance and confession, led to reconciliation. No issues were aired, no voices raised. The Holy Spirit had been at work. –*LaVerna Klippenstein*

Holy Spirit, dwell with us.

Devotional 5

[Mary] will bear a son, and you are to name him Jesus, for he will save his people from their sins. —Matthew 1:21

On Good Friday, the pastor projected a picture of Rembrandt's portrayal of Jesus on the cross, surrounded by an assortment of interested and curious bystanders. When asked to place myself somewhere among the onlookers I mused, "I want to be closer, rather than farther away."

We do not normally turn to the Passion for inspiration when we think of Jesus' birth. Yet this text evokes Jesus' lifelong mission, to bring salvation. Emmanuel, the other fitting name given to Jesus, means "God is with us." Our liberation from sin comes through God's coming among us.

In Jesus' birth, ministry, death, and resurrection, God has lived among us as "Savior" and "Emmanuel."

In the drama of Jesus' advent and ministry, where do I place myself? Am I a disinterested bystander keeping my distance? Or am I standing nearby closely identified with him? –*Ken Seitz*

God with us, we accept your salvation and invite your presence in our lives.

Devotional 6

. . . and they shall name him Emmanuel, which means "God is with us." —Matthew 1:23

When I was born on January 21, 1950—two months premature, a tiny 3½-pound package of human life—my parents named me Dorothy Jean. This name came from two aunts: Dorothy Elizabeth, my mother's sister, and Velma Jean, my father's sister.

The meaning of my name is a special gift. Dorothy (the feminine form of Theodore) means "gift of God." And Jean (the feminine form of John) means "God is gracious." What better gift could I receive than the confession of faith reflected in this name? My life itself is nothing other than the gift of God. And the God who has gifted me with life is gracious. Here are name, confession, and calling sufficient for a lifetime. –*Dorothy Jean Weaver*

God of many names, thank you for your gift of life and love. As your daughters and sons, we know that you call us "Beloved."

Devotional 7

But [Joseph] had no marital relations with her until she had borne a son; and he named him Jesus. —Matthew 1:25

Matthew's portrayal of Joseph's patience illustrates a profound trust in God's plan. Joseph and Mary did not consummate their marriage until Jesus was born. How patient Joseph was!

Very recently our family waited as my aged father completed his life. He could no longer eat or drink. He had lived a full life and was confident of his eternal resting place.

He constantly pointed upward toward a small sign above his bed that read, "Perhaps Today." The sign referred to Christ's second coming, but now it had added meaning. Dad was patient. We also needed to be patient as we waited.

What are you waiting patiently for? Possibly a loved one to commit to Christ, a child to make better lifestyle choices, an injustice to be addressed, or a church issue to be resolved?

Be patient in your waiting, for those who wait on God won't be disappointed (Isaiah 49:23). –*David Wiebe*

Patient One, our time is in your hands. What would you have us learn while we wait on you?

Provocative preacher

MATTHEW 3:1-12

Opening

Matthew 3 introduces us to a charismatic prophet with a bold style and riveting message. People flocked to the wilderness to hear John's preaching. More than just onlookers, they heeded his message of repentance by confessing their sins and being baptized in the river.

Think of the charismatic preachers you have heard. What made them effective speakers? Would you travel a distance to hear them? What message would convict you to change your actions or attitudes?

Understanding God's Word

John the Baptist cuts a large figure in the world of the New Testament. All four Gospels agree that Jesus' ministry begins with John, and that Jesus submits to his baptism. Jesus' first followers were followers of John first. Jesus himself, and the community he founded, adopt the practice of baptism.

John's appearance is bizarre and his message is for repentance and about fire and denunciation. Yet multitudes make the difficult journey to hear him, including many of the religious elite. What draws the crowds? Is it to mock a fanatic living in the desert or is it out of a longing for the return of the prophet Elijah?

Connecting with God's Word

The messenger
John's appearance in Matthew's Gospel is told in language that echoes Israel's faith, history, and expectation. John comes out of the desert as Israel did. He wears camel's hair and a leather belt, just like Elijah, the Jewish prophet (2 Kings 1:8). He eats a simple diet of locusts and wild honey.

John's ascetic lifestyle suggests a connection with the Essenes, a monastic community that withdrew from mainstream Jewish society and lived near the

For the leader

1. Pray for open eyes, open ears, and open hearts as you explore this text together.

2. Ask the group to imagine being there, in the wilderness, waiting to see and hear John the Baptist. After a moment of silence, read the text slowly. Then ask participants to tell how they experienced the story: Where were they in the crowd? How did they receive the message?

Dead Sea. They disapprove of the priesthood and temple worship in Jerusalem and develop a strict set of standards and rituals. While John believes, as they did, in the imminent judgment, the need for Israel to repent, and use a ritual washing, he departs from the Essenes in several ways: He calls everyone to new life, not just a select few; he uses a missionary strategy rather than complete withdrawal, and baptism is once-and-for-all, not a life of ritual washing.

Like Elijah, John is a lone voice calling in the desert, with a message that appeals to the masses.

- Had you lived back then, would you have joined the masses to hear John preach? Explain your answer.
- How does a messenger's dress or background (or age, race, gender, politics) affect how you hear her or his message? Think of someone whose message surprised you because they did not fit your criteria.
- The expression "a voice crying in the wilderness" describes someone who seems alone in expressing a deep conviction in some matter. Tell of an issue or a setting in which you felt like a lone voice. How can you make your voice heard?

The message

John's ministry is linked directly to the prophecy of Isaiah. As Matthew tells it, Jesus is the Lord who is coming, and John prepares the way.

John comes with a simple message that will become Jesus' own: "Repent, for the kingdom of heaven is near." To repent is to "turn around" or "return," confessing and renouncing the sins of the old life. And the "kingdom of heaven" is God's initiative, not a human accomplishment. Matthew's characteristic use of "heaven" probably reflects the Jewish reluctance to utter the name of God.

Confession of sins led to immediate baptism in John's ministry. For Matthew, baptism in the Jordan may symbolize starting over by reliving Israel's crossing into the Promised Land, or washing away unrighteousness, or symbolically passing through the judgment that God is about to unleash.

The public ritual of baptism signaling a change in outlook is not enough. In attacking the official religious leaders, John emphasizes their need to show evidence that their minds have been transformed or they, too, will be consumed in the coming fire. Nor can they hide behind their ancestry. It is a popular idea of the time that Abraham's merits were sufficient to cover the shortcomings of his descendants. John will have none of this. It is the good fruit of the repentant life that will survive God's judgment.

- John's message has three components: repentance, baptism, and actions. What are the dangers if we uphold only one or two parts?
- Is John the Baptist's message still relevant today? How would you re-word his message in contemporary language?

Our response

For John, the appropriate response to his message is a two-step act. Step one is repentance and confession of sins, which is acknowledged by baptism. Step two is the step that lasts a lifetime, actions that are "in keeping with repentance."

The response is also communal. The "kingdom of heaven" is intimately connected to the repentance of God's people. For John this clearly means to think as God thinks and to get with God's program, which is not for the faint of heart or for couch potatoes. Repentance leads to baptism, which is nothing less than ordination by God to be God's agents of healing and hope in a desperate and dangerous world.

"God has now acted," John is saying. "God's reign has already come near. So it's time for you to respond."

- The "kingdom of heaven" implies communal life. Repentance and baptism are about living faithfully as God's people. Give examples of when the church community has needed to acknowledge its sinfulness and repent.
- How can the church examine and re-order its life?
- Actions give visible evidence of a repentant life. What such evidence do outsiders see when observing your group or congregation? What else can you do?

Closing

1. Sing a hymn based on this session's text, such as "Prepare the way of the Lord," number 14 in *Sing the Story* (Scottdale, Pa: Mennonite Publishing Network, 2007).

2. For the next session, think about your own baptism and its impact on your life.

3. Give a sending blessing to each other: *The way has been prepared. Walk in it and be transformed by it.*

Devotionals

Devotional 1

*In those days John the Baptist appeared in the wilderness of Judea, proclaiming . . .
—Matthew 3:1*

Elie Wiesel tells the story of a Jewish prophet in a Russian village who daily went to the village streets and proclaimed his message. At first, small crowds of curious onlookers gathered. As he continued to preach, however, his audience dwindled to nothing. Still he kept on, day after day.

A boy approached him. "Why do you preach?" he asked. "Can't you see no one is listening to you?"
"I'm afraid that if I don't keep preaching," the prophet replied, "I may begin to listen to them."

A prophet deals with two dangers: the fear that the message will go unheard, and the possibility of huge success.

John emerges from the wilderness and is faced with the danger of overwhelming success. But his refuge was the same as for the Russian village prophet: a dogged loyalty to his message, and a fierce and relentless pointing away from himself to Another.
–Leonard Beechy

Faithful God, give me the courage and resilience to bring your message of hope and healing to those who cross my path.

Devotional 2

Repent, for the kingdom of heaven has come near. —Matthew 3:2

I hear the familiar morning sounds in my home in a rural Nicaraguan village, and I imagine the setting of this story. I picture myself as a slightly confused observer, attracted to the strange, charismatic preacher. What did John mean when he said, "The kingdom of heaven has come near"?

I imagine people making their way to the Jordan—rich, poor, healthy, disabled. As they approach John for baptism, they speak earnestly and he listens carefully. Suddenly, he turns to the religious leaders and demands, "Bear fruit worthy of repentance!"

I wonder if John fully understands what he is saying? Does he realize that the birth of his cousin, Jesus, represents the entrance of God's kingdom into our world?

God takes the initiative to come close to us, hoping that we, in turn, will draw close to God, by accepting God's gift of unconditional love. *–Susan Classen*

God, when I fall into the trap of thinking I need to earn your love, remind me that I am totally loved by you.

Devotional 3

The voice of one crying out in the wilderness: "'Prepare the way of the Lord, make his paths straight.' " —Matthew 3:3

Christmas preparations shift into high gear during December, with all the shopping, baking, decorating, hosting, and visiting relatives. I can get so busy that reflection on

Christ's coming slips into the background. In the end, will the results of my frenzied Christmas preparations have any meaning, or will they melt down like candles and disappear with the trash?

John, too, was caught up in preparation. He was preparing the way of the Lord by preaching to the crowds who flocked to the desert. He told them to reorder their lives, to put out of the way those things that hindered them from receiving the kingdom of God that had now "come near."

In all the seasons of my life, I want to reorder the flurry of preparations so that I can celebrate God's reign, which Christ's birth brought into the world and into my life. —Ferne Burkhardt

God, I want to prepare my heart for Christ to enter in.

Devotional 4

Prepare the way of the Lord, make his paths straight. —Matthew 3:3b

Friends and family send Christmas cards with greetings such as, "Happy Holidays," or "Good News of Great Joy." I have yet to receive a card that said, "You brood of vipers!"

John the Baptist comes as a jolting, disturbing voice as we prepare for the peace and wonder of Christ's coming. We would just as soon skip over his harsh words of warning. We'd rather not hear his cries to repent. We'd rather go shopping or bake some cookies!

Advent is about preparing the way for Jesus to enter anew into our lives. Even though we live two millennia later and Christ's Spirit lives among us throughout the year, we do well to prepare for a new visitation of God among us. Each year we are confronted with the invitation to prepare for new directions and welcome the gift of God-with-us. —Jayne Byler

Challenge me, Lord, where I need to straighten out my life, where I need to prepare anew for your presence.

Devotional 5

The voice of one crying out in the wilderness: "'Prepare the way of the Lord . . .'" —Matthew 3:3b

I was at a crossroads in my life, struggling with career and relationship issues, when I stumbled upon a small retreat center on a desert mountain in New Mexico. In the serenity of this setting, the wilderness spoke to my inner being.

In the tender green shoot pushing up through the hard soil, I heard, "Take heart, the struggle gives you strength." In the quiet of a morning stroll, I heard, "Be still and know that I am God." In the majestic moonlit night sky, I heard, "My peace I give to you."

The voice I heard in the desert was the voice of the divine, calling me to make room for new possibilities, to prepare my heart for a new pathway that would lead to a deeper, more intimate relationship with God. Sometimes it's those dry, deserted places in our inner landscape that provide the richest source of growth. —Eleanor Snyder

Loving God, when we find ourselves in the wilderness, may we hear your encouraging voice.

Devotional 6

Bear fruit worthy of repentance . . . I baptize you with water for repentance, but one who is more powerful than I is coming after me. —Matthew 3:8,11a.

A striking figure, John warned those whom he baptized that his baptism was a first step, that repentance was a process, and that he was preparing the way for someone more powerful.

We celebrate the coming of this more powerful person, Jesus, at Christmas.

While washing windows one day, I recalled what my mother taught me long ago. Washing windows is a two-step process, she explained. First, use a sloppy wet cloth to apply plain water, no soap. Second, and more importantly, dry the window with a soft, lint-free cloth until there are no streaks. I would tire of all the vigorous polishing and sometimes omit the second step. The window looked clean when wet; however, when the sun shone against it, the streaks were revealed.

The daily practice of Jesus' teachings is like the second step in window cleaning, for it continues the process of repentance.
–Janet Toews Berg

Lord, I want to feel your power in this daily work of repentance.

Devotional 7

Do not presume to say to yourselves, "'We have Abraham as our ancestor'" . . . God is able from these stones to raise up children to Abraham. —Matthew 3:9

In my congregation we have a tradition that those who travel bring back a stone from a place they have visited. The stone is taken to the courtyard and placed among the others around our Peace Pole. The stones surround the Peace Pole, which looks as if, by some miracle, it had grown from them.

John the Baptist looks at the stony ground of the Judean wilderness and proclaims, in the face of his audience of Pharisees and Sadducees, that God can make from these stones children of Abraham. That means us. From the first verse, Matthew's Gospel wants us to remember that Abraham was ancestor of many nations, including Gentiles. And to become children of Abraham, according to John's preaching, we must do one very un-stone-like thing: We must bear fruit. John means the good works of love in action. And he means us.
–Leonard Beechy

Thank you for the miracle of grace by which you call me your child. Show me today how I can produce the fruit of loving action.

Declaring identity

MATTHEW 3:13-17

Opening

Today's scripture text tells of Jesus' baptism in the Jordan River. Take a moment to reflect on your baptism experience, and then share briefly with a partner or with the group:

- How old were you?
- Where, how, and why were you baptized?
- What did it mean for you then?

Understanding God's Word

We learn in Matthew's first two chapters about Jesus' supernatural conception and Joseph's decision to raise him as his own son. After a surprising and unexpected visit from magi, the family made a harrowing escape to Egypt. Later they moved to Nazareth where Jesus was raised.

Years pass. When we meet Jesus in Matthew 3, he is an adult and ready for public ministry. But before he begins, he will be "ordained" by God for his mission. His baptism becomes his ordination for ministry.

For the leader

1. Bring a small bowl of water.

2. Sing, listen to, or read the words of a baptism song from your hymnal. Pray for the presence of God's Spirit in your midst.

3. Read and act out Matthew 3:13-17. Ask for 3 readers: narrator, John, Jesus, and bystanders (all others). Have everyone read the voice from heaven (verse 17).

Connecting with God's Word

John baptizes Jesus (3:13-15)
In the first part of chapter 3, John is busy preaching, calling people to repentance, and baptizing those who confess their sins. Then Jesus shows up on the scene. Like his Jewish compatriots Jesus comes from Galilee to the Jordan seeking baptism by John. John is completely confused. He has been proclaiming one who is more powerful than he, one for whom he is unworthy to carry out even the humblest task. This one will baptize, not with water, but with the Holy Spirit and fire. Surely this person, Jesus, does not need to confess his sins like all the others and receive John's water baptism.

So why has he come? John puts the question to Jesus directly and Jesus' response sounds a note that will ring throughout his upcoming ministry: "Let it be so now; for it is proper for us in this way to fulfill all righteousness" (15). This is all about God. This is what it means, for Jesus and for John, to be faithful to God and to carry out God's will. "Go ahead and do it," Jesus says to John. And John does so.

- John baptized Jesus in the same way he did others who sought him out. How do you think John, Jesus, and other witnesses perceived this act?
- Explain the difference between water baptism and baptism by the Holy Spirit as you would to a new believer.
- Think of a time when you ministered to someone who seemed spiritually more mature. How did this experience impact you?

God affirms who Jesus is and equips him for ministry (3:16-17).
Just as Jesus emerges from the water, God puts on a heavenly display that leaves no question about who Jesus really is and what Jesus' mission is all about. In an extraordinary divine three-step, God (1) "opens" the heavens, (2) the Spirit of God descends "like a dove" onto Jesus, and (3) "a voice from heaven" (clearly the voice of God) proclaims, "This is my Son, the Beloved, with whom I am well pleased."

This is Jesus' ordination for ministry. Jesus has shown solidarity with his people in coming to the Jordan as they have done. He has "fulfilled all righteousness" in receiving the waters of baptism from John. And God now affirms Jesus' identity and equips him for his upcoming ministry.

Jesus is God's messianic agent, chosen to carry out God's purposes on earth and to exhibit God's ultimate reign in the world of competing powers and authorities. As God's beloved Son, Jesus is invested with, and empowered by, that Spirit for his ministry. Jesus is faithful to God's call and God breaks open the heavens to pronounce a cosmic "Yes!"

- What amazes you about this baptism scene?
- Jesus was an adult when he was baptized where he received both his identity and calling in a public setting. What are some advantages of waiting until adulthood to be baptized?
- How do you experience God's pleasure?

Our baptism as empowerment for ministry

Not only is baptism the calling of God to a task that is larger than life, but also, it is God's affirmation and empowerment for that calling. In baptism God claims each of us as beloved children and empowers us for ministry through the gift of the Holy Spirit.

Baptism is an important step on a lifelong faith journey. Baptism "ordains" us for ministry no matter what our vocation, no matter what our age. We are called to use our gifts in a way that points others to God so they, too, can claim their status as beloved daughters and sons of God.

- Reflect again on the significance of your baptism. What does your baptismal experience mean for you now? How has this act transformed your lifetime?
- What is the ministry to which God has called and ordained you? Identify a gift of ministry that you have. Name it aloud and claim it.
- Baptism assumes being accountable to a Christian community. We can help each other discern our calling and gifts of ministry. Identify a gift of ministry or calling that you see in another person in the group.

Closing

1. Claim your identity as a beloved child of God. Pass a bowl of water or go to a central location. As you dip your hand into the water and gently rub it on your forehead or hand, say aloud, "I, (name), am God's beloved daughter (or son)."
2. Give a sending blessing to each other: *Live out your baptism with confidence and joy, for God delights in you.*

Devotionals

Devotional 1

Then Jesus came from Galilee to John at the Jordan, to be baptized by him. —Matthew 3:13

For most people, it was an ordinary Sunday evening church service. However, for a few of my peers and me, it was far from ordinary. This was our baptismal service. We would confess our faith, receive the waters of baptism, and be welcomed as members into the church community.

We stood at the front of the church and said yes to our baptismal vows. We knelt as the bishop poured water on our heads. Then he took us by the hand and raised us to our feet with the powerful words of Paul about walking "in newness of life" (Romans 6:4).

I was 12 years old. I knew with certainty that God had called me. I responded, imagining this to be a "once and done" event. Little did I know that my baptism was the first step. Years later, I know that it was the one that transformed a lifetime. –*Dorothy Jean Weaver*

Thank you, dear God, for walking with me every step of the way.

Devotional 2

A voice from heaven said, "This is my Son, the Beloved, with whom I am well pleased." —Matthew 3:17

When I was a child, my grandmother gave me a nameplate with my name, which means "beloved." She said to me, "We don't take our identity from who we are or from whom others think we are, but from whom we think others think we are."

When we feel vulnerable to the opinions of others we can deal with it by saturating our minds with the messages of the most important opinion-maker. "See what love the Father has given us," Scripture tells us, "that we should be called children of God; and that is what we are" (1 John 3:1-2). We may know this verse, but has its truth moved from our heads into our hearts? If not, it is more like a plaque on a wall than a lovingly embraced part of our identity.

Repeat these words aloud: "I am God's beloved." Let this affirmation guide you daily. –*Aimee Reid*

I rest in your care, like a child in a parent's arms. Cradle me in your love, God.

Devotional 3

A voice from heaven said, "This is my Son, the Beloved, with whom I am well pleased." —Matthew 3:17

When Jesus was baptized, he heard words of love and assurance. God spoke these words before Jesus began his ministry, before he did anything that could be interpreted as earning God's love. Jesus was able to fully receive God's love. I, on the other hand, need to be reminded frequently that God loved me even before I was born.

JoAnn, my Mennonite Central Committee co-worker in Nicaragua, has a special gift with children. She intuitively recognizes children who need assurances of being loved. A painfully shy little girl, Nubia, came to return a book. Her voice shook as she courageously read aloud to JoAnn. JoAnn sat close, listening attentively, and then she praised her for reading so well. Nubia's face glowed.

May our faces glow from the knowledge that we are loved and pleasing just because we are God's daughters and sons. –*Susan Classen*

Gracious and loving One, help me to relax into my identity as your beloved child.

Devotional 4

A voice from heaven said, "This is my Son, the Beloved, with whom I am well pleased." —Matthew 3:17

It's a smile I will never forget. It was our 8-year-old son's first piano recital. I was nervous as he sat down to play. He looked down at the keys, then looked right at me and smiled. "Don't worry, Mom. You'll be proud of me," that smile seemed to say. And he did well, and I was proud. I congratulated him later.

When Jesus was about to begin his ministry, he came to John for baptism. "My beloved Son," the voice said from the open heaven. What a way to begin his ministry!

Henri Nouwen suggests that the greatest gift we can give each other is the gift of "belovedness." Many voices say, "You are no good; you are worthless." But we can counter with, "You play the piano well" or "I enjoy your company." It may bring smiles you will never forget! –*Edna Krueger Dyck*

Loving God, as your beloved child, I want to recognize and affirm others who need to receive the gift of belovedness.

Devotional 5

A voice from heaven said, "This is my Son, the Beloved, with whom I am well pleased." —Matthew 3:17

I imagine the voice from heaven as an audible voice in words clearly understood by everyone who witnessed the baptism of Jesus.

Don't you sometimes wish you heard an audible voice from heaven? When you're not sure how to respond in a difficult situation, or faced with a tough decision? When feeling confused and uncertain, how comforting it would be to hear and know the sure voice of God!

Yet, I wonder if we would recognize that voice. Would we dismiss it as our imagination or as an unusual roll of thunder? God's voice already speaks in many different ways—through the words of Scripture, in quiet moments of prayer, in the words of a sermon, through the counsel of a friend, in the midst of a busy family life, on a hike up a mountain. Do we recognize God's voice when it comes to us in these and many other ways? –*April Yamasaki*

Lord, help me to recognize your voice today, and to respond in ways that are pleasing to you.

Devotional 6

A voice from heaven said, "This is my Son, the Beloved, with whom I am well pleased."
—Matthew 3:17

We were playing a board game with our adult children. At one point, my husband and I exchanged some affectionate teasing. I noticed the expression on our son's face, and realized that our words and gestures had delighted him.

In the story of Jesus' baptism we witness two remarkable exchanges. One is between Jesus and John. Their conversation reveals openness and trust. It includes humble protest, persuasion, and consent. The second is the moment when Jesus emerges from the waters of baptism, when he senses the Spirit's anointing upon his head, and hears the loving affirmation of the One who sent him.

These short but significant encounters warm and inspire me. I want to be like John, trying to understand and consent to God's purposes. I want to be in the company of Jesus, where I too am a Spirit-filled and beloved child, able to hear "I'm pleased with you." –*Dora Dueck*

Lord, make my interactions with others be honest and warm this day.

Devotional 7

A voice from heaven said, "This is my Son, the Beloved, with whom I am well pleased."
—Matthew 3:17

In his baptism, Jesus identified with those who came to be baptized, repenting of their sins. Our baptism, in turn, identifies us with Jesus and his task of pointing others to God.

When I face a decision with my deep personal convictions guiding me, it is easy to follow the right path. If I want Jesus in my life, I know I have to develop my relationship with him. Praying and reading God's word are appointments that I must keep in order to nurture this relationship.

We are given opportunities to help others and serve the church that demand careful consideration. Where shall I use my gifts? What does God want me to do? I know I am God's well-loved child. I also know that God is pleased with whatever service builds God's kingdom. And so today I hear the invitation, "I want you to keep your appointment with me." –*Edith Ratzlaff*

Lord, thank you for the many opportunities to use my gifts in loving service to you.

Finding true happiness

MATTHEW 5:1-12

Opening

Do you consider yourself a happy person? What makes you happy? What blessings have you received this week? Mark the following "common sense" blessings you find attractive. Which ones are more difficult to let go of?

1. How fortunate are those who have their lives under control and do not need anyone else.

2. How happy are those who avoid situations that expose them to grief or suffering.

3. How happy are those who pay back folks who hurt them.

4. How fortunate are those who hunger and thirst after money and the things it can buy.

5. How fortunate are those who are generous only to folks who deserve it.

6. How happy are those who function out of mixed motives.

7. How fortunate are those who have the good sense to turn away in the face of conflict.

8. How happy are those whom everybody likes all the time.

These blessings, of course, are the opposite of what Jesus taught. Can you imagine how the people in Jesus' time reacted to teachings directly opposite to what they would have expected?

For the leader

1. Bring a variety of translations of the Beatitudes. Have on hand art supplies, paper, and pens.

2. Read the Beatitudes, one at a time, using several versions. Pause briefly after each verse to allow time for reflection, or take time for discussion after reading each beatitude.

Understanding God's Word

The teachings and sayings of Jesus are very important to Matthew, so much so that they are given prominence at the beginning of Jesus' ministry. These teachings form the Sermon on the Mount (chapters 5-7).

The Beatitudes (5:3-12) are not demands or orders, but statements of an upside-down reality that flies in the face of common sense. They are inklings of what the reign of God, or as Matthew calls it, the "kingdom of heaven," sounds and looks like. They invite Jesus' first disciples, and us, into it.

Connecting with God's Word

Eight sound bites about the reign of God (5:3-12)

The Beatitudes are inter-connected, like stepping stones. Living the first one helps us enter into the second, and so on. We are truly blessed, happy, fortunate and to be congratulated (Greek word makarioi) if we live into them, for that means we are embodying the reign of God.

Here's how we might describe each beatitude for today's disciples:

1. (5:3) Rather than striving for self-reliance and self-sufficiency, Jesus says in effect: "Congratulations if you know you don't have it all together, if you know you can't go it alone or if you recognize your need for God and for a supportive community. You are ready to enter a new territory where the supposedly weak and the supposedly strong help each other."

2. (5:4) Rather than avoiding or hiding our suffering, we acknowledge and feel the suffering both within ourselves and in our world. We seek God's consolation for ourselves and offer it to others. Those who lament the brokenness of creation will eventually find comfort.

3. (5:5) Rather than protecting our own happiness by paying people back, we demonstrate a gentle spirit. This does not mean being a doormat or timid. The Greek word stresses the notion of gentleness, a characteristic that even strong, decisive people have. Blessing comes from waiting for God to act and not seeking vengeance ourselves.

4. (5:6) Here Jesus seeks to remind disciples of hungers and thirsts which can (and by implication, which cannot) be satisfied. However, a desire for a right relationship with God will be satisfied.

5. (5:7) Jesus responds here to the false belief about who is deserving. This blessing lifts up those who demonstrate mercy with both compassion and forgiveness. They will receive mercy in return (presumably from God and other people). We know that God has mercifully reached out to us beyond our deserving.

6. (5:8) Purity of heart is the focus of this beatitude. While we moderns tend to associate the heart with feelings, it was considered to be the nexus of thought, will, and choice in Jesus' day. Thus, to have a "pure heart" was to have a clear focus, which meant a heart directed toward God. "Seeing God" thus envisions communion with God

7. (5:9) Those who actively seek and pursue peace reveal God's character. Active peacemaking transforms broken relationships into reconciliation. The "reward" of those who live this way? People will observe, "There walks a true child of God!"

8. (5:10-11) Will disciples who live out these beatitudes gain the approval of others all the time? Far from it. More likely they will receive active opposition. If you're persecuted because of your right living, then you're already living in the territory of God's reign, so rejoice and be glad.

- Consider the idea that the Beatitudes are interrelated and serve as stepping stones. Does one lead to the next one, and so forth? As you see the interconnections, share your insights about the kind of disciples Jesus is calling us to be.
- The Beatitudes are not imperatives but do imply a moral demand. Do they describe character or conduct? Do you think they are meant as a present reality or a future claim?
- Could you adopt the Beatitudes as your standard of happiness? Explain your answer.

Living out the vision

- Choose one beatitude for further reflection. Put it in your own words. Use poetry, art, or a story to illustrate what it means for you.
- Affirmations increase our happiness quotient. On slips of paper, write out a brief blessing or affirmation to give to others in the group or in your family. You, too, will experience true happiness as you extend blessings to others.

Closing

1. Name one characteristic of true happiness that you would like to experience this week.

2. Sing, "Blest are they," number 94 in *Sing the Journey* (Scottdale, Pa: Mennonite Publishing Network, 2005).

3. Give each other this blessing: *As happy followers of Jesus, may God bless you and make you a blessing to others.*

Devotionals

Devotional 1

He began to speak, and taught them, saying "Blessed are..." —Matthew 5:2

Writer Philip Yancey casts light on the Beatitudes when he writes: "Blessed is Lazarus (the poor in spirit), and the Good Samaritan (the merciful), and the Publican and the Prodigal Son (those who hunger and thirst for righteousness), and the mongrel guests at the wedding feast (the meek)."

Yancey suggests that Jesus was a "master of contrarian thinking." Jesus teaches that true greatness grows from unconventional soil. Yancey sees the greatest wisdom in the patient at a leprosarium in India; in a civil rights worker who worked out his theology in a jail cell; in a priest who took a vow of poverty and now serves the severely disabled. Yancey says he once pitied these people. Now he envies them.

To live the Beatitudes is a far cry from what our culture teaches us. It takes courage to go against the stream of culture, and to defy its hold on our lives. *—Marvin Hein*

Dear Teacher, give me courage to live the upside-down life you taught us about.

Devotional 2

He began to speak, and taught them, saying: "Blessed are the poor in spirit." —Matthew 5:2-3

She was working at the bagel shop, like a morning memo on the Good Life. She lightly tended to the tables, chairs, counters, and me. She had a crisp dignity I found riveting.

As the diners' fast-track intensity swirled about her, I realized: She is the one Jesus was talking about—the poor, the meek, the hungry, the merciful. Without doubt she struggled to make ends meet, yet she had the bearing of abundant nobility.

I felt an impulse to gavel the distracted customers to order, and say, "Please, sister, tell us the story of the secret you know!" But the winter dawn replied, "It's not the secret she's found. No, it's the secret that has found her—that Sermon on the Mount secret that pursues us all."

And so, I passed silently on my way, a hunger roused within, but braced by the common majesty of Jesus' secret about the Good Life. *—Jonathan Larson*

"In simple trust like theirs who heard ... the gracious calling of the Lord, let us, like them, without a word, rise up and follow thee!"
—John Greenleaf Whittier

Devotional 3

Blessed are the meek, for they will inherit the earth. —Matthew 5:5

A strange and wonderful phenomenon occurred during the Christmas season. When some families went to the department store to make a payment on their layaway plan, they discovered that the entire bill had been paid. Seeking more information, they learned that someone who wished to remain anonymous had paid the entire amount, with no strings attached. What a welcome surprise to the families. Christmas was especially joyful that year.

Jesus congratulates people who are humble and gentle. They are "close to the sacred earth" as Philip Newell interprets this verse. Usually we think that people are humble because they lack power and status. But those who treat their status and power lightly also demonstrate humility when they are willing to give away what they have, joyfully, and with no strings attached.

In God's realm, an attitude of humility brings happiness as we give and receive what God has to offer. *–Eleanor Snyder*

Gentle One, may we experience the joy and strength that comes with a humble spirit.

Devotional 4

Blessed are those who hunger and thirst for righteousness, for they will be filled. —Matthew 5:6

In the newspaper I saw a picture of a Haitian woman making mud cookies to sell as food. The cookies, though brown, were not a dressed-up name for dark chocolate cookies; they were formed from dirt, salt and vegetable oil. The high global price of rice and beans had led to desperation. Few of us have experienced such hunger. Yet crippling hunger and poverty have always been a reality in our world.

In this beatitude, Jesus uses human experiences to describe our longing for God. To paraphrase, "Those desperate for a right relationship with God will be special guests at God's banquet."

The Beatitudes link opposite human experiences. Hunger is paired with satisfaction; grief is linked to comfort; the poor in spirit are going to inherit the kingdom of God; and those persecuted will have great rewards. These bite-sized statements of kingdom values open our eyes to God's surprising ways. *–Larry Hauder*

God of the hungry, the thirsty, and the poor of spirit, lead me in meeting the human and spiritual needs that I see today.

Devotional 5

Blessed are those who hunger and thirst for righteousness, for they will be filled. —Matthew 5:6

Our congregation enjoyed a bus trip to Pennsylvania to see sites and watch the play Behold the Lamb. The production portrayed the life of Jesus, emphasizing his teaching ministry, including the Beatitudes.

On a stop at the Ten Thousand Villages headquarters, teenagers noticed the Latin American prayer on a wall: "Lord, to those who hunger give bread, and to those who have bread give hunger for justice."

We wondered what hungering for justice and righteousness means for us. What changes might we make in our thoughts and actions? We concluded that hunger for the rights of others is an outcome of following in the path of God's righteousness.

"I wish," said one participant, "that I would spend more time 'thirsting' for righteousness and not be too quick to move to the application of the principle."

As the conversation continued, a senior reminded us of Jesus' promise that such hungering and thirsting would be satisfied. –*Doug Snyder*

Lord, move us to hunger for justice and righteousness today.

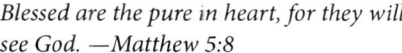

Devotional 6

Blessed are the pure in heart, for they will see God. —Matthew 5:8

In his book Heaven is for Real, Todd Burpo recounts the story of his son. Little Colton claimed to have gone to heaven during emergency surgery and tells his family about spending time with Jesus and God. Colton reported back that Jesus and God love everyone. He often repeated how much Jesus loves the children.

The openness, innocence, and honesty of children can point us to God. We do well to pay attention to their "God-talk," and to the awe and wonder that they see in their surroundings.

Pure hearts are clean and clear. There is a focus, an intentionality to live the life God calls us to with integrity. When our hearts are clear so is our vision. We will see God in relationships that are genuine and loving. We will see God in all of life–children, nature, prayer and community. We will see the Living Presence everywhere. –*Eleanor Snyder*

Dear God, clear our hearts, so that we may see you in ourselves, in others, and in the world.

Devotional 7

Blessed are the peacemakers, for they will be called the children of God. —Matthew 5:9

The prison guard opened the door to a meeting room where two men waited to speak with the two who entered. They discussed the disturbing increase in young men being incarcerated.

The groups represented the towns of Elmira, Ontario and Elmira, New York. The discussion provided an idea for a new peacemaking initiative that would put certain offenders on probation and have them meet weekly with a trained volunteer from the church community.

The project grew. Three years later, a second idea developed for the offender to be placed on probation and to make restitution for their actions. A volunteer would go with the offender to meet those were victims of the actions.

Thirty years later there are similar victim-offender reconciliation programs worldwide. The original driving force of the movement was a pair of God's children captured by the beatitude, "Blessed are the peacemakers." –*Doug Snyder*

Thank you, God, for small initiatives for peace that grow like mustard seeds in our communities. What innovative thoughts are you planting in me today?

Salt, light, action!

MATTHEW 5:13-20

Opening

Metaphors are word-pictures that tell us about something that may be hard to describe. Biblical writers often used metaphors to describe God, God's reign, and the church. Name some from memory: "God is like…."; "God's reign is like…"; "The church is like…"

What metaphor best describes your faith community for you? Explain your choice.

Understanding God's Word

This text is a part of the Sermon on the Mount. Immediately after Jesus delivers the Beatitudes, Matthew has Jesus plunging into other sayings about conduct. Using metaphors of salt and light, Jesus describes the kind of visible community of disciples he expects of his followers.

In the next part of the teachings, from Matthew 5:17 through chapter 7, Jesus ties his message to Jewish law. Matthew wants to make it very clear that Jesus came to fulfill the law and the prophets, not destroy them.

For the leader

1. Bring a small bowl containing salt and a small source of light: flashlight, penlight, or candle.

2. If you have access to a hymnal, sing or read the words of the song, "You are salt for the earth," number 226 in *Hymnal: A Worship Book* (Scottdale, Pa: Mennonite Publishing House, 1992).

3. Pray for enlightenment as you explore the salt and light metaphors for discipleship.

4. Read the text in three sections. Read verse 13 several times as you pass around a small bowl with salt, inviting participants to taste it. Similarly, read verses 14-16 as you pass around the light. Pause, and then read verses 17-20.

Connecting with God's Word

Salt-seasoning (5:13)
Many sermons stress the various attributes of salt: as seasoning, preservative, medicine, melting agent, and, in excess, destroyer of life. Jesus isn't concerned with followers turning into a mineral. The stress is on "tastiness" or "zest" in the symbolic relationship. If believers lose their tang, their aliveness, their excitement at being in relationship with Christ, the relationship withers. They might as well be pillars of salt.

Eugene H. Peterson in *The Message* suggests that we are here to be "salt-seasoning that brings out the God-flavors of this earth." Wherever we are, we are showing what God's reign actually tastes like. We are drawing people to Jesus in comfort and in hope.

- In an age of low-salt diets, is this metaphor still an appropriate one? Explain your answer.

- How is your congregation (group or family) "salt-seasoning" in your neighborhood?

- What are some ways we can maintain a "tangy" relationship with Christ? What can we do to restore our saltiness?

Light-bearing (5:14-16)
Jesus does not command us to be salt and light; rather he is simply naming the reality of who we are. The relationship we are offered with Jesus is not just to make us feel good. We are called into relationship so that we can light up the world. To be light for the world means that we "bring out the God-colors in the world," according to *The Message*. When the rest of the world sees our behavior, our character, our spirit, and our liveliness, they should see Jesus, and thus bring glory to God. Wherever we are, we are showing what God's reign actually looks like. We are drawing people to Jesus, the bright light to the world.

- When the world looks at your congregation (or group or family) do they see something different? What do you hope they are seeing?

- What kind of light is the church projecting in the world: the flame of a match, the beam from a flashlight, or the bright lights of a city on a hill?

- How can you bring out the "God-colors" in the world around you so that others are compelled to give glory to God?

Law-abiding (5:17-20)

Some people who heard the radical teachings of Jesus were quick to accuse him of wanting to drop the sacred teachings of their past. Jesus, however, did not come to abolish but to fulfill what was written and taught. He came to deepen and widen the law so that its true intention comes to the fore. He came to create a community that lived out God's will in word and action.

While Jesus sets his teachings over and against some aspects of the Old Testament law, his words line up with the goals to which the law and the prophets pointed, namely, to love God and your neighbor. Jesus did not intend to set the Old Testament teachings aside but to line up his teachings with the heart of the "gospel" of the Old Testament. Those who follow Jesus must live out the Scriptures in the way that Jesus interprets them, as is illustrated in verses 21-48.

- Try rewriting or "translating" these verses into contemporary language. What words best convey Jesus' teaching about the law for us here and now?
- According to Jesus, the scribes and Pharisees may not have lived out their beliefs adequately. To become great in God's reign meant to live obediently and be an example to others. Which Christian teachings do you find harder to practice than to "preach"?

Closing

1. Play with more metaphors. Think of another image that reflects the message of today's text. Use this formula: a) name the image; b) illustrate with an example; c) give a negative example; d) end with positive note. Offer this to the group. For example: You make a warm comforter for others. Such blankets are meant to provide warmth on a cool night. They do no good tucked away in a closet or stored in a blanket box. No, their comfort and security warm both body and soul in a tired world. This humble service of our hands warms the heart of God.

2. Actions speak louder than words. Our actions matter. Name one action that would tell the world that your community is made up of salt-seasoning, light-bearing, law-abiding disciples of Jesus Christ.

3. Give each other this blessing: *Be like salt and light in a world that needs to taste God's grace and see God's love.*

Devotionals

Devotional 1

You are the salt of the earth. —Matthew 5:13

I have been a victim of the classic saltshaker blooper, in which one inverts the shaker only to have the lid fall off. The result is an alarming pile of salt where only a few sprinkles were desired. At these times I've tried to scrape off the pile and proceed with my meal, but it never works. The seasoning has become too strong to appreciate.

Sometimes we Christians misunderstand the purpose of being like salt in the world. We can focus on trying to be very salty, with little consideration of the effect it might have on others. An overly strong dose of salt is not pleasant.

Salt is enjoyable only when dispensed in appropriate, well-directed ways. When we are like salt, Jesus said, it inspires people to praise the God we serve. When our actions and words are a blessing to others, then the seasoning we sprinkle will indeed be welcomed and savored. –*Philip Wiebe*

Lord, I want to be like salt and light to those around me.

Devotional 2

No one after lighting a lamp puts it under the bushel basket, but on the lampstand, and it gives light to all in the house. —Matthew 5:15

It was my boyhood chore in northeast India to light the kerosene lamps and distribute them around the house. I learned a lot about lamps as I handled mantles and wicks, filled fuel reservoirs, and cleaned the glass globes and vaporizers.

When the lamps were all lit, I'd carry them to various corners of the house. Each person had what light they needed.

This experience helps me understand Jesus' image of the community of faith, except that in Jesus' vision the lamp lights the whole house.

Let our households of faith be one-room houses. Let them have common lights—the soft lamps that burn gently in the corners, the powerful lights that reach even into the rafters, and the brilliant ones by whose light we read the sacred stories. And let there be ample room in that mingled light—that common light—for all who come in from the night. –*Jonathan Larson*

Let my light shine all through the house.

Devotional 3

Let your light shine before others . . . —Matthew 5:16

Have you ever experienced an "Aha!" moment, a time you had a fresh insight? As both a learner and a teacher I've had such moments of inspiration. There's a feeling of amazement when a new realization emerges and I "get it." There's a sense of satisfaction when something I've said or done has helped someone else "see the light."

We are called to be light-bearers, shedding light on God's ways, bringing out the "God-colors in the world" (The Message), so that others see the light. Like a city that is lit up by many lights, the Christian community works together, offering glimmers of light to its surroundings.

God, the Divine Illuminator, expects us to be little pieces of light, lighting the world through authentic word and deed, helping each other find our way. *—Eleanor Snyder*

Light a candle and pray: Giver of light, may your light within me be reflected in my daily life.

Devotional 4

Let your light shine before others, so that they may see your good works and give glory to your Father in heaven. —Matthew 5:16

When my family traveled to a remote camp in Washington State's Cascade Mountains, I hoped to enjoy the unpolluted brilliance of the moon and stars. Unfortunately, clouds and the lights from our camp obscured the heavens on the nights that I stayed up late.

The presence of night does not guarantee that we will see the brilliance of the moon and stars. Similarly, the presence of adversity does not guarantee that our Christian lights will shine. Doubts and worries can cloud the brightness of God's love, or busyness and exhaustion tempt us to ignore celestial wonders.

Jesus doesn't glorify suffering's darkness for its own sake but for the opportunity it presents to reflect and appreciate the light of God's love. When we clear away distractions, fears, and doubts, we transform nights of suffering into opportunities to experience awe and peace. And we enable others to experience them as well. *—Leslie Hawthorne Klingler*

Great Light of all life, shine your love on me and help me to reflect your light to the world, especially in the darkness of night.

Devotional 5

Do not think that I have come to abolish the law or the prophets; I have not come to abolish but to fulfill. —Matthew 5:17

Children are raised with rules, and children often resent them. Parents hope that eventually an inner desire to do good replaces simple obedience.

The 16th century Anabaptists regarded the Old Testament as a preamble to the real thing: the good news of grace through Jesus Christ. They studied and preached mostly from the New Testament, especially the Sermon on the Mount.

They were right to affirm that Christians are set free from the legalism of the Old Testament, but they were wrong in thinking that one can become a transformed person without acknowledging and appreciating one's roots. That is what Jesus emphasized when he said that he had come to fulfill the law, not abolish it.

The question for us is, are we still like children, or have we grown up? Do we hear this as a command, or as a glad and welcome whisper within us? –*Peter J. Dyck*

Lord, I want to grow up spiritually and be like Christ in following the spirit of your law.

* * * * * * * * * * * * * *
Devotional 6

Whoever does [these commandments] and teaches them will be called great in the kingdom of heaven. —Matthew 5:19

One summer I took part in a seminar on Shakespeare taught by a Jewish woman. She told me that she had recently read the Gospels in preparation to teach biblical literature. She said, "It isn't easy to follow Jesus, is it?" I agreed. I also let her know that I find joy in doing it.

Reading the Gospels made my professor recognize the faithfulness of this Jewish man Jesus and the high standard he has for his followers.

As Jesus preached the Sermon on the Mount his listeners may have thought they were hearing something completely new and different. However, Jesus assured them that living in God's kingdom does not negate the commandments. He taught that he came to fulfill the law.

Jesus' love for God and his love for others included the ultimate sacrifice of his own life. He challenged us to follow his example of obedience, to be faithful hearers and teachers.–*Janet Gehman*

Thank you, God, for Jesus' example and for the joy that comes with daily walking your way.

* * * * * * * * * * * * * *
Devotional 7

Unless your righteousness exceeds that of the scribes and Pharisees, you will never enter the kingdom of heaven. —Matthew 5:20

Studying a foreign language takes getting used to. At first, instead of your educated self, your limitations make you sound like a child at best and a fool at worst.

Mastering a language takes time. It may begin with memorizing verb endings, but it doesn't end there. You have to speak, sing, pray, and explain until the language rules are second nature.

Just as we might overdo grammar drills and never get around to conversation, so the Pharisees were so obsessed with legal details that they neglected true righteousness. As grammar describes language patterns, so the law describes how God works in the world.

True righteousness is not just a matter of not breaking the law, but of adopting the behavior of the Sermon on the Mount: loving enemies, not worrying and judging, praying for God's kingdom.
Like using a foreign language, it's worth the effort. –*Mary Raber*

May I have the courage to let go of my fears and experience the freedom of true righteousness.

Redefining the rules

MATTHEW 5:21-48

Opening

From young up we've learned to live by rules. In his book, *All I Really Need to Know I Learned in Kindergarten*, Robert Fulghum suggests that wisdom is found on the playground of kindergarten children. What were some of those playground rules you remember as a child, either spoken or unspoken? Which of these rules still apply? Which rules have you tweaked or discarded as an adult?

There is the saying, "Rules are meant to be broken." When is it appropriate to break a rule? Give an example of someone who broken a societal rule which led to positive change?

The Sermon on the Mount (Mathew 5–7) records Jesus' teachings on various questions of faith and behavior. In this session, we examine Jesus' way of redefining the rules of his day.

Understanding God's Word

Matthew's Gospel makes it clear that Jesus came to fulfill the law of the prophets, not abolish it. The sacred teachings of the past are still to be valued. Jesus puts a new spin on how to interpret these teachings. In fact, Jesus calls for something more from his followers, even more than what is expected from the religious leaders.

For the leader

1. Mark a continuum on the floor using masking tape or rope long enough for everyone to stand on it. On the left end, place the word, FAIL; on the right side, PASS WITH HONORS.

2. Pray for openness to the Spirit's convictions as you explore Jesus' interpretation of the rules to live by.

3. Ask six readers to read the text by section: verses 21-26; 27-30; 31-32; 33-37; 38-41; 43-48.

In six sets of antitheses, Jesus selects an Old Testament law and illustrates God's intent for it. Each saying begins with a version of, "You have heard that it was said." Then Jesus redefines it for his community, saying, "But I say . . ." In this act Jesus claims divine authority.

Connecting with God's Word

Do not be angry (5:21-26)
In this first antithesis Jesus quotes the sixth commandment, "You shall not murder" (Exodus 20:13), adding that those who kill will be subject to a trial. He follows with the not-so-obvious comment that it is also against the law to be angry with another and to speak harsh words against that person. So act quickly to be reconciled, because uncurbed anger leads to more drastic acts. Jesus exposes the root of violence, the inner systemic cause.

Do not lust in your heart (5:27-30)
Here Jesus recalls the seventh commandment, "Do not commit adultery" (Exodus 20:14) and draws on the tenth commandment, "You shall not covet" (Exodus 20:17). The law is meant to protect the legal rights of marriage and ensure a stable and trustworthy marital relationship.

Jesus expands the law, going a step further. Adultery does not begin in the neighbor's bedroom but in the heart where lust arises. Again, Jesus probes the underlying first step that leads to adultery if it is not curbed. Using exaggerated language, Jesus urges his followers to take whatever means necessary to avoid adulterous behavior.

Do not divorce, except . . . (5:31-32)
By Old Testament law, a man is permitted to divorce his wife if she "becomes displeasing to him because he finds something indecent about her" (see Deuteronomy 24:1-4). Upon a "bill of divorce," the marriage is dissolved and both are free to remarry. This law caused many debates among the rabbinic teachers of Israel. Jesus interprets this law in a way that limits male power— it is unacceptable for a man to divorce on any other grounds than adultery. Jesus speaks for healthy marriage relationships.

Do not swear at all (5:33-35)
When a promise made between two people is broken, mistrust begins. Thus arose the practice of swearing "by God," invoking God as a witness. Since Jews did not want to utter God's name, they chose other immovable objects, such as "heaven" or "Jerusalem" by which to swear an oath. Jesus indicates that all of these substitutes are connected with God, and so the problem of swearing "by God" still remains. Oaths only increase suspicion. If God

honors a person's promise through a simple yes or no, then the same should suffice for person-to-person relationships.

Do not resist an evil person (5:38-42)
Here Jesus deals with the "law of retaliation" (Exodus 21:23-25; Leviticus 24:20). This law protects a victim from insult or injury with a rule for compensation or retribution. It also protects the one who inflicted the injury by ensuring that the punishment fits the crime. Jesus goes beyond this time of restricted revenge. The way to get "back at" someone is through non-violent resistance. A disarming gesture is a first step on the road to redemption.

Love your enemies (5:43-48)
"Love your neighbor" (Leviticus 19:18) tells people to love their fellow Israelites. While some psalms lash out at the cruelty of enemies, there is no Old Testament commandment to "hate your enemies." Jesus may be quoting hearsay. Regardless, he expands the rule of love to the enemy, even telling his followers to pray for them. Children of God make no distinction between love for friends and attitude toward enemies. This is what it means to be perfect, that is, to be all that God intends.

- Are these teachings still as radical today as they were in Jesus' day? Explain your answer.
- Which teachings do you warmly agree with and comply with? Explain your answer.
- Which teachings do you find difficult or prefer to resist? Explain.
- Are these teachings realistic for the Christian church only or for society as well?

How are you doing?
This text calls us to live by Jesus' redefined rules. How are you doing as a congregation or group? Find your place on the continuum where you would rate the group in terms of faithfulness to each of Jesus' teachings. Explain your position. Overall, how are you doing?

Closing

1. Which teaching do you need to spend more time pondering in order to apply it to your life? For accountability, tell the group.
2. Give each other a blessing: *Be faithful and true to the teachings of Jesus.*

Devotionals

Devotional 1

Come to terms quickly with your accuser while you are on the way. —Matthew 5:25

The evening meal in the dining hall was over. I had just spoken to the several hundred brothers and sisters of the Bruderhof, a Christian group that lives communally. A man suggested we go for a walk while the others remained to confess any wrongdoing they had done during the day, asking for forgiveness. I was told that this was done every evening and only "among ourselves," following the words of Paul: "Do not let the sun go down on your anger" (Ephesians 4:26).

What a wonderful idea to wipe the slate clean daily, to go to sleep with a clear conscience! Admit your wrongdoings and ask for pardon. How different our lives would be if we took that first difficult step of reconciliation.

I believe the Bruderhof are on to something that not only boosts good mental health and relationships, but is also biblical. Jesus expected his disciples to practice confession and forgiveness. *–Peter J. Dyck*

Give me courage, Lord, to confess and apologize when my conscience accuses me.

Devotional 2

First be reconciled to your brother or sister, and then come and offer your gift. —Matthew 5:24

What is remarkable about Jesus' instruction on the Good Life is that understanding among one another takes precedence over–indeed, is a condition for–worship of God. So urgent is this order that Jesus counsels abandoning the flow of worship–imagine! Prayers suddenly broken off, choral anthems left hanging in mid stanza, preachers stepping out of sermon and pulpit–all to seek restored kinship before proceeding with the order of service.

I have never witnessed this, but I yearn that we might be such a community, that I might be such a disciple and worshipper of God. Let the entryways to our meetinghouses be furnished with the instruments of reconciliation. Let no one pass into the place of worship without opportunity to pause first and take up that fiery stone with brother or sister–to make an end of estrangement so that we may worship in freedom and joy. *–Jonathan Larson*

Forgiving One, may I experience the gift of reconciliation that I have received from God and freely extend it to others.

Devotional 3

First be reconciled to your brother or sister, and then come and offer your gift.
—Matthew 5:24

It's easy to feel guilty. If I'm angry with someone and she has no idea that I'm so irritated, do I really have to go to her and ask for forgiveness? What if it comes as complete surprise? Then surely I've opened a can of worms!

A closer look shows that Jesus asks us to go, not to those we are angry with, but to those who are angry with us! When I know that a relationship is strained because of something that I've done, Jesus asks me to stop what I'm doing and go to them. But even that is difficult! It means changing my behavior.

Ultimately, Jesus' way will result in mercy. Instead of living with guilt I can seek forgiveness. Bypassing the usual gossip, avoidance, or third-party interventions, mercy prevails when we approach these things head on, with a spirit of humility.
–Jill Landis

God, give me courage to seek forgiveness when I have hurt another.

Devotional 4

But I say to you, do not swear at all.
—Matthew 5:34

To swear can mean using obscene language or taking an oath. We are to shun both kinds, but this reference is about oath taking.

During the Second World War I faced Judge Burges in Manchester, England, for refusing to become a soldier and for refusing to take the oath. I was a young volunteer with the Mennonite Central Committee, working with war victims, especially children and older people. Graciously Burges allowed me to "affirm," but pointed out that the penalty for perjury would be the same as if I had taken the oath.

If we take truth-telling seriously, then we accept the early Anabaptist belief that "word and deed are one." It means that when I say "peace," I also am a peaceful person; when I say, "forgive," I am a forgiving person; and when I say "love," I am a loving person.
–Peter J. Dyck

Lord, help me to be your authentic disciple.

Devotional 5

You have heard that it was said . . . But I say to you . . . —Matthew 5:38-39

Jesus and his audience knew the law and its allowances for retaliation. But Jesus offered a new message: Don't act like an adversary or insist on settling the score. Instead, surprise the offender with a response that defuses the conflict.

Several years ago Dan Snyder, a professional hockey star, died when his teammate, Dany Heatley, smashed his Ferrari into a wall at a high speed. Heatley faced the prospect of 20 years in prison.

Dan's father, Graham Snyder, asked the judge for leniency. He declared that taking away Dany's future would only compound their grief. The impressed judge ordered probation and driving restrictions instead of jail. He also ruled that Dany make speeches to young people about dangerous driving.

Bewildered reporters headlined the forgiving spirit of the Snyder family. Graham's response, however, had deep roots.

He had learned alternatives to revenge and retribution from an initiator of the Victim Offender Reconciliation Program. —*Ferne Burkhardt*

Open our minds, hearts, and wills to respond creatively when we encounter ill will or injury.

Devotional 6

But I say to you, Love your enemies and pray for those who persecute you.
—Matthew 5:44

A freshly minted word, "abductive" comes from the root abduct meaning "to carry off illegally, to kidnap." As a teacher, storyteller, and preacher, I have been provoked by Jesus' abductive method of teaching. It is an approach so drastic, so daring, and so subversive that settled norms and conventional wisdom are dismantled at a single stroke. All familiar, self-serving landmarks are swept clean away by a moral earthquake.

There seems to be no other way to get to that high ground that Jesus calls the kingdom. We have been abducted to an impossible realm where weary bitterness has become sweet kinship. Adamant hatreds have melted away and conventional enmities of clan, culture, creed, and class have given way to love.

If ever heaven were to speak to us, we would hear this abductive message: Love your neighbors well. Love your enemies, too! —*Jonathan Larson*

Lord, may we strive for higher ground in our love for others.

Devotional 7

Love your enemies and pray for those who persecute you. —*Matthew 5:44*

A story is told about an Arab woman living in Jerusalem. In 1948 her family fled ahead of the Israeli invasion. In 1976 she returned to Jerusalem to find her old home occupied by a Jewish widow living alone.

When she explained her wish to see her home, she was invited in. She said, "When my husband and I left, we grabbed our belongings and fled, but our son was not with us. Each thought the other had taken him."

The Jewish woman felt faint. Her husband, an Israeli soldier, had entered this house during military operations in 1948. He had found the child, and was permitted to keep both him and the house.

As the two women talked, a 30-year-old Israeli soldier entered the room. "This is your son and my son," she said.

The women decided to live together in that house. Love for enemy attained a new definition.

Lord, give us the courage and imagination to love as you love.

Practicing piety and trust

MATTHEW 6:1-15; 25-34

Opening

Money talks, and prayer matters. Take a few moments to jot down your reflections on your practices with your finances and your prayer life.

1. Which charities do you support financially? How do you respond to a street person asking for spare change? What motivates you to give away your money?
2. When did you pray this week? For what did you pray? How does your prayer life draw you closer to God? What is your motivation for praying?
3. In the group share a brief response to one of the questions above. When it comes to motivation, is it easier to talk about your finances or your prayer life?

The Scriptures for this session address our motivation for living a righteous life based on the teachings of Jesus that we find in the Sermon on the Mount.

Understanding the Word

After Jesus reinterprets the laws that deal with righteous living, he moves to a discourse on the meaning of genuine piety. While much of Matthew 5 is about right relationship with our fellow humans, Matthew 6 explores the actions that stem from our relationship with God. Practicing piety means "doing righteousness."

For the leader

1. Bring paper and pens for the opening exercise.
2. Ask one person to read Matthew 6:1-8. Have the group prayerfully read verses 9-15 together. Ask another person to read verses 25-34.

Jesus teaches that an orientation toward God means that we put our trust in something beyond ourselves. Instead of being preoccupied with our station in life, we can trust that God cares and provides for us.

Connecting with God's Word

Charitable giving and prayer (6:1-8)
Jesus assumes that his disciples will carry on the common practices of almsgiving (6:2-4), prayer (6:5-15), and fasting (6:16-18), practices which have carried a prominent place in Jewish faith. These examples of practicing piety are not in question, but our motive is. Are we doing them for God or to attract others' attention? There are consequences when we do the right things for the wrong reasons.

Jesus uses exaggeration when he speaks of contributing financially to the needy. The word *hypocrite* refers to actors in a play. Jesus cautions against making a performance out of our giving. It's not that we should go out of our way to hide what we're doing, but that our giving is for God to see and recognize, not others.

As for prayer practices, the same logic applies. In other words, "Don't show off to your fellow believers to demonstrate the sincerity of your prayer life." Nor should you go on and on out of anxiety that God will not respond, because God already knows what you need.

- What might Jesus say to us about current fundraising practices for charitable purposes?
- To pray regularly helps focus and reorient us to God. How do both spontaneous and scripted prayers (from prayer books) help us to focus our prayer life?
- What prayer habits work best for you?

A model for prayer (6:9-15)
The Lord's Prayer includes three petitions which ask God to act on God's agenda, and three petitions which ask God to care for our needs.

In verses 9-10, we seek God's nature and intention to be revealed in the world, a world that does not revolve around us. We find ourselves transported into a new territory which Jesus referred to as the kingdom of God (or of heaven). These petitions take us there, as do all the Beatitudes. Prayer is about first inviting God's kingdom to expand, and then asking in trust that our own needs will be met as we give ourselves to this journey with God.

In verses 9-12, we petition God to care about the physical necessities of our lives. To ask for what we really need to sustain our lives saves us from anxiety and from frantic striving. God provides for right relationships with

God and with others, and so we can seek forgiveness with confidence. If we forgive those who do wrong to us, we are saved from resentment and revenge. If we allow God to forgive us we are saved from brooding endlessly over our own sins or trying to cover them up. Verses 14-15 speak of the reciprocity between the way we respond to the misdeeds of others and the way God responds to our own.

In verse 13, we pray that God will save us from losing our way in the fog or from stepping off a precipice. It's meant to enable us to make the choices we need to make, even in tough situations.

- Share your history with the Lord's Prayer. Do you find it life giving? Explain.
- How should this prayer be used in homes, churches, and public settings?

Don't worry—God provides (6:25-34)

Jesus repeatedly calls his followers not to worry about basic necessities of life, such as food, drink, clothes, and shelter. Birds daily collect food, as they need it. And flowers don't help God sustain their life, yet they live and are beautiful. These analogies remind us that worrying does not contribute to solving a problem, nor can it lengthen one's life. Trust in God is the corrective to worry.

Jesus emphasizes God's familiarity with our circumstances and God's ability to sustain life. The challenge to people of faith is to see all of life as a purposeful existence with God. Trust in God instead of fretting about the future is the prescription that Jesus offers his followers. It is a call for purposeful activity that builds relationship and moves us beyond excessive introspection that can lead to despair.

- Define "need" and "luxury" in a way that would make sense to rich and poor, urban and rural, North American and Third World.
- We may be someone who wrestles with anxiety, doubt and worry. How can our families and congregations provide environments of trust and patience that contribute to their and our long-term emotional health?

Closing

1. Praying the Lord's Prayer is a dangerous undertaking. We might catch God's vision and begin to dream God's dreams. Then we may need to adjust our own visions, dreams, and wants accordingly. Pray this prayer together, with conviction.

2. Give each other a blessing: *Give generously, pray passionately, and trust fully in the One who knows you intimately.*

Devotionals

Devotional 1

When you give alms, do not let your left hand know what your right hand is doing, so that your alms may be done in secret. —Matthew 6:3-4

On occasion we have been in need, wondering when we could next afford to buy groceries. One morning we awoke to find a brown paper grocery bag stuffed with groceries outside our door. We did not try to discover the source of this gift. Rather, it served to remind us how God's people strengthen and encourage.

There is a righteous sense of delight when we secretly do something unabashedly good for someone else! But let's also recognize that it is possible to do righteous things to impress others, rather than glorify God.

Who do you know who could benefit from a secret act of mercy, an encouraging note? Who could be strengthened by a bag of groceries, or flowers? The possibility for acts of mercy is as infinite as the Creator of mercy. Pray for a pure heart, asking God to direct your attention to those in need, then begin scheming. *—Craig Morton*

God of grace and mercy, use me to shed the light of your glory on someone who needs to see it.

Devotional 2

When you are praying, do not heap up empty phrases. —Matthew 6:7

In church, we all have our prayer preferences. Some appreciate a prayer that's written ahead of time. Others prefer a spontaneous prayer. The Spirit can lead both public prayers.

When I'm asked to lead in a public prayer, I need to pray alone first. My public prayer develops in the solitude of my own "prayer closet." It includes a lot of silent spaces. It's redundant, as I repeat a phrase such as "Open my heart, Lord." My prayer requires editing before it becomes part of public worship. But it is from the heart.

If a prayer comes from my "inner closet," whether in private or public, planned or spontaneous, God will be honored. It all comes back to where my heart is. *—Sandra Drescher-Lehman*

God, thank you for making the way for each of us to come to you in a personal and unique relationship.

Devotional 3

Pray then in this way. —Matthew. 6:9

There's a bumper sticker that instructs, "Question Authority." Rebellious spirit that I am, my response is, "Oh, yeah! Says who?" There are times when I need someone to tell me what to do, where to go, and how to do it. At these times, I just want to "Ask Authority."

Prayer seems almost instinctual. We are "hardwired" for a relationship with God. Seeking God in despair, and offering praise in moments of wonder, are common experiences among people. However, we need to be taught how to pray in a meaningful focused way, for the things that really matter. To whom do I pray? Why? What for? What does prayer do to me and for me?

So much is said by Jesus' simple introduction, "Pray then in this way." In this short exhortation, Jesus is saying, "This is important." *–Craig Morton*

Loving teacher, may your Spirit intercede for me and teach me how to pray.

Devotional 4

Your kingdom come. Your will be done, on earth as it is in heaven. —Matthew 6:10

"O Canada! Our home and native land." These opening lines of the Canadian national anthem are a tribute to the national pride of Canadians.

Stored in the same memory cells as my national anthem are the words to the Lord's Prayer. The prayer begins on an intimate note by addressing God as our parent. Then I recognize that I am part of God's kingdom. In addition to being a Canadian citizen, I'm also a citizen of God's realm.

The Pacific, Atlantic, and Arctic Oceans mark Canada's territory. What are the parameters of God's realm? The Lord's Prayer, the anthem of God's kingdom, defines an infinitely larger scope. God's authority is broader than any country's borders or ethnic divisions. God reigns over the universe.

When I feel a sense of camaraderie with my fellow citizens, I will give thanks for those who are also God's kin. *–Lynn Graham*

Ruler of all, remind me of my loyalty to you and of my calling to be a good citizen in your world.

Devotional 5

Give us this day our daily bread. —Matthew 6:11

The crowd Jesus addressed included people suffering from the injustice flowing from a select few. The high temple taxes, coupled with taxes extracted by foreign rulers, devastated their capacity to feed themselves and their families. They lost their land ownership and eked out an existence as debtors. The petition for daily bread thus addresses a life-and-death reality for these Galilean peasants.

In this prayer, Jesus connects the petition for daily bread with the petition for forgiveness. We are called to trust God for the provision of bread, but a life sustained by this bread has as much to do with forgiveness as it does with the physical nourishment that bread provides. While we may experience physical hunger, we can be grateful for God's providence.

Let's not miss the importance of the spiritual bread of forgiveness. Enemy love and forgiveness are the substance of this bread. —*Jon Yoder*

Giver of Bread, as I sit down to eat today, I thank you for your life-giving nourishment: food and forgiveness.

Devotional 6

If you forgive others their trespasses, your heavenly Father will also forgive you. —Matthew 6:14

There's a joke about a driver being pulled over by a police officer. She asked the officer what the problem was. The officer smiled apologetically and told the woman she was free to go.

"Then why did you stop me?" the woman asked.

The officer replied, "I noticed how angrily you reacted when another driver cut you off a few miles back. Then, when I noticed all the Christian bumper stickers on the car, I figured it was stolen!"

The funny story points to a larger reality that Jesus alludes to. As Christians, we receive grace and mercy from God that transforms us into new people. We don't behave in the same old ways. We are called to extend mercy to those who offend us, thus living out our new identity. If we will allow it, God's grace and mercy can flow through us into the world. —*Regina Shands Stoltzfus*

Forgiving God, teach me to share your generous love and forgiveness with all I meet.

Devotional 7

I tell you, do not worry about your life, what you will eat or drink, or about your body, what you will wear. —Matthew 6:25

When our family moved to a new farm, we borrowed money to make the down payment. Even though we felt God leading us we had to watch every penny. Youth from our former church came to visit. After a hot dog roast we wanted marshmallows, so I gave my wallet to a volunteer to buy some.

The next morning, I looked for my wallet and found it in the remains of the fire. My driver's license and other important papers could be replaced, but my carefully allotted grocery money was now reduced to ashes.

I struggled to find ways to feed my family with the resources I had. We were thankful for our garden, fresh farm milk, and the meat in our freezer. The unexpected gifts from friends and neighbors proved to us that God could indeed provide for our needs. —*Ruth Smith Meyer*

Merciful God, help me to trust you for my needs and use me to answer the prayers of others.

Meeting human needs

MATTHEW 25:31-46

Opening

There is a story told of a group of cantankerous rabbis who were always fighting. One day they were told that one of them was the Messiah visiting in disguise. Their attitudes and actions changed remarkably. Since they didn't know which one of them was the Messiah, they began to treat each other with respect, and the bickering stopped.

Think of the people you live and work with. Think of the strangers you encountered in the last few days. What opportunities did you have to respond to someone in need? How did you respond? If you could "do it over again" what would you do differently if you believed you were serving Christ?

Understanding God's Word

The parable of the sheep and goats is found at the end of the final discourse of Jesus in Matthew 24-25. The theme is the end of time. The parable does not address questions of how the end will come or how the resurrection might happen. It focuses simply on the reality and event of judgment at the end of time, and the basis on which people will be awarded with eternal life or condemned to eternal punishment.

A gathering of the nations for judgment is a popular way of depicting the end of the age in Jesus' culture. Judgment occurs around the throne of God,

For the leader

1. Pray for insight and understanding as you wrestle with the meaning of this parable for today.

2. Ask someone to read this parable with expression. Invite the others to listen. Pay attention to those who are surprised in the parable. Imagine what would have surprised those who were listening to Jesus telling the parable. What surprised you?

with the Son of Man presiding as judge. In the drama, the people of the nations are divided, just as a shepherd separates sheep from goats.

Connecting with God's Word

Blessing the sheep (25:31-40)
The sheep are rewarded because of their service to others. Six deeds of mercy are presented in this parable: providing for people who were hungry, thirsty, strangers, poorly clothed, sick, and imprisoned.

These blessed ones respond in amazement and surprise because they are not sure they have done anything spectacular. But such acts of hospitality bring a commendation from God. Their service reflects their commitment to God. This service is not mere friendliness to neighbors or family members who would be equals in matters of economics and status. In this parable, service means reaching beyond the scope of normal relationships to the arena of outcast and disenfranchised people.

- Which deeds of mercy are most comfortable for you to do? Which ones would stretch you? Explain your reasons.
- As governments reduce their direct involvement in social programs, what is the church's response?
- How do you think God will judge those who do righteous deeds without having had the opportunity to know Christ?

Judging the goats (25:41-45)
The goats in the parable are reprimanded for not serving other people. Following the example of the sheep's court case, the goats are condemned for not helping people who were hungry, thirsty, strangers, poorly clothed, sick, and imprisoned.

The goats are surprised at their plight. They are not thieves, adulterers, lawbreakers, or atheists. They are people who neglected their call to meet human need. They were spiritually blind to the claims of God in their lives. For that, they will be sorely judged.

This text highlights the eternal consequences of behaviors, attitudes, and spirituality. The call to serve others is at the core of Jesus' call to faithfulness.

- Where are the blind spots of our life experiences that keep us from seeing the obvious needs of others?
- The parable makes the basic point that God holds us accountable for our conduct. While God's overall objective is to redeem and restore, the reality is that some people are unwilling to seek justice and do acts of

compassion. How do you believe God's desire to redeem and restore fit together with God's judgment?

For reflection and response

We North Americans generally enjoy a prosperous lifestyle and an abundance of material goods. As a response to our prosperity, the church often calls people to service that demonstrates the love and compassion of Christ for others. The church also calls members of congregations to faithful stewardship of financial resources to sustain its mission.

The mission challenge continues to be one of finding a balance between inviting others to accept the gospel message and meeting the physical and social needs of the world. Mission work includes evangelism, humanitarian assistance, and advocacy of justice for those who are oppressed.

- Examine your congregation's budget allocations. What percentage is used for mission endeavors? Are you being good stewards of your financial resources?

- How would you rate your congregation in finding a balance in doing mission work?

- In what ways can this parable help your congregation make decisions about its worship, education, stewardship, and mission life?

Closing

1. According to Menno Simons, true evangelical faith does not lie dormant; rather it clothes the naked, feeds the hungry, comforts the sorrowful, and shelters the destitute. Share one way you can practice true evangelical faith in the coming days.

2. Give each other a blessing: *May you see the face of Christ in everyone you serve.*

Devotionals

Devotional 1

Then the righteous will answer him, " 'Lord, when was it that we saw you hungry and gave you food, or thirsty and gave you something to drink?' " —Matthew 25:37

What I find most compelling in this parable is the genuine surprise of the righteous that they had served Christ with their deeds. In that measure, they are exactly like the unrighteous: they never recognized the incognito Christ. They were all utterly oblivious to Jesus present in the guise of the famished, the parched, the alien, the naked, the infirm, and the captive. The righteous did these things out of such gratitude, and with such complete conviction, that it was the least they could do.

    This is the authenticating mark of what it means to be righteous: to be completely unaware of one's saintliness. Let our deeds of mercy be marked by such persuasive, compelling oblivion. Let them remain a secret both to us and to others. *–Jonathan P. Larson*

Compassionate One, fill us with your love and show us how best to serve our neighbors.

Devotional 2

Then the righteous will answer him, " 'Lord, when was it that we saw you hungry and gave you food, or thirsty and gave you something to drink?' " —Matthew 25:37

In Jesus' parable, both the rewarded and the condemned are surprised. Those who receive gracious commendations for their deeds have no idea what they did to be recipients of a reward. The reward is sweeter because it is unexpected.

    I've had a foretaste of that sweetness. When I told friends that I had been diagnosed with acute leukemia, my earthly life was predicted to last only a few months. A most gratifying thing has been the unexpected response from hundreds of people who remember events or conversations where my life touched theirs. I do not recall many of them.

    As I anticipate meeting the Savior, I am thrilled to think about the rewards for works we don't even recall. I'm glad I have no list to present; every reward will be a surprise. *–Marvin Hein*

Lord, help me to live in such a way that on judgment day I shall hear "Well done" for deeds I never dreamed had won your approval.

Devotional 3

Just as you did it to one of the least of these who are members of my family, you did it to me. —Matthew 25:40

Our task was to plan a worship service celebrating the kingdom of God. The conference administrator said that she saw God's reign in plans to plant more churches. The pastor said we could invite people from different countries to read the same Scripture in their native language. The homemaker suggested that God's rule was evident in the food deliveries by members to families in crisis. The artist saw the image of a bare tree slowly filling out with beautiful leaves. The song leader reminded us to express the joy of God's reign through music.

We went our separate ways, on the lookout for places where God's reign is evident. Out of this simple nudge to notice came a rich litany of God's kingdom, singing, celebrating, sharing, filling our senses, and filled with joy all over the place! In God's kingdom, nothing is too small to do.
–Sandra Drescher Lehman

God, I celebrate the smallest gift of my time, words, or attention, as things that can help to grow your kingdom.

* * * * * * * * * * * * * *
Devotional 4

Just as you did it to one of the least of these who are members of my family, you did it to me. —Matthew 25:40

It was common for people in need to knock on our church door requesting a cup of coffee or financial assistance. The challenge was to distinguish truth from fiction. We tried to meet real needs.

One afternoon I was enjoying a quiet study time when a knock at the church door interrupted me. I begrudgingly opened the door to find a single mom requesting help with groceries. My desire to continue studying was stronger than my desire to help. I refused her request and watched her dejectedly walk away.

The Spirit convicted me. Had I just turned Jesus away at the door of the church? I ran after the woman and apologized for my failure to take her request seriously. I went with her to the store to get groceries.

I learned the valuable lesson of not only studying the Word but also of acting in obedience to it. –*Michael Dick*

Sensitize our hearts, dear God, to the needs we encounter today, and give us willing hands and feet to serve.

* * * * * * * * * * * * * *
Devotional 5

Just as you did it to one of the least of these who are members of my family, you did it to me. —Matthew 25:40

"Who is my neighbor?" According to Martin Luther King, a neighbor is anyone, anywhere who needs help. It may be a person who lives next door or someone miles away.

How often have I been insensitive to others' needs, walking away from my neighbor when a kind word, a smile, a listening ear, or an honest compliment would lift their spirits? Whether the needs are for food, clothing, shelter, understanding, or love, I want to graciously reach out to that neighbor.

Jesus cared deeply for others, especially those who were disenfranchised. –*Jocele Meyer*

May I look to Jesus as my model and follow suit—quietly, but with diligence and determination.

Devotional 6

Then they also will answer, " 'Lord, when was it that we saw you hungry or thirsty or a stranger or naked or sick or in prison, and did not take care of you?' " —Matthew 25:44

My friend became a pen pal to a death-row inmate. As the inmate's final days drew near, my friend wrote letters to government leaders and justice groups, seeking to have the prisoner's sentence commuted.

When the inmate lost his final appeal, my friend grieved. As I shared his grief, I became aware of my own personal loss. I also had had an opportunity to visit a prisoner but had turned it down.

My friend found Jesus in prison through the life and spirit of Christ in his inmate brother. He stepped deeper into God's kingdom with each letter.
We were separated by our different answers to the same question: Lord, when did we see you? He had the courage to take a small step in the right direction. I did not.

God used my friend to remind me that only one step is needed to come back to God. *–Adam S. Yoder*

Nudge me, dear God, to find you in the "wrong" places and meet you in the "least of these."

Devotional 7

I tell you, just as you did not do it to one of the least of these, you did not do it to me. —Matthew 25:45

At age 13, I was hospitalized with severe abdominal pains. I was admitted to a huge hospital and lay awake the first night, imagining horrors. Told that in the morning my innards were to be completely emptied, I pictured the slate of tests the doctor had described to me. To make matters even more unpleasant, the screaming man who was admitted to the next room at midnight frightened me.

A nurse explained that the man had been struck full force in the belly by a goat. She tried to comfort him as best she could.

Ever since my hospital stay, I've lived with two strong convictions. First, goats can be nasty and second, people need to receive attentive, focused care when hurting, lonely, and afraid. I don't want to be a goat, knocking someone's gut, perhaps contributing to extreme discomfort. To be a sheep, I need to give care. *–Doug Schultz*

Lord, may I live in such a way that will draw others to your own absolute kindness.

CPSIA information can be obtained at www.ICGtesting.com
Printed in the USA
BVOW012128150412

287607BV00005B/3/P

9 780836 196399